INVADERS AND SETTLERS

Contents

Introduction

Two thousand years ago, <u>Britain</u> was very different from the country you know today. The people who lived in Britain then were called Celts. They lived in wooden huts in small villages. Surrounding the villages were thick forests full of wild bears, wolves and boars.

Most Celts were farmers. They grew all their own food. They were good at making things from wood and iron like weapons and chariots.

▲Maiden Castle is a famous Celtic fort. This is what it looks like today.

This is what a Celtic hut may have looked like inside. The walls of the hut were made of branches twisted together and covered with dried clay.

The Celts lived in groups called tribes with their own king or queen. The tribes often fought each other. Some tribes built forts on top of hills which were very difficult to attack.

We Celts didn't read or write any books, so you don't know much about us.

LOOKING AT EVIDENCE

Forts give us clues about how the Celts lived. These things also help us to find out more about the Celts.

A helmet.

A shield.

A cooking pot.

3

The Romans

Two thousand years ago, in the country we now call Italy, lived the Romans. They were very different from the Celts. They lived in big cities, like Rome, full of huge buildings made from stone. There were shops, baths, temples and theatres.

Try and find Rome on a map.

1▶ Julius Caesar was the first Roman to attack Britain, in 55 <u>BC</u>. He left after only a few weeks.

   Caesar invaded Britain again, a year later. He won a few battles but did not stay long enough to conquer Britain.

2▲ Nearly 100 years later, Emperor Claudius sent a large army to conquer Britain. Some Celts like Queen Boudicca fought hard against the Romans.

3▼ Boudicca killed many Romans but was finally defeated. She drank poison rather than be taken prisoner.

The Romans soon ruled much of southern Britain.

4

Why did the Romans invade?

What a waste of money! Britain wasn't worth conquering.

I wanted to win fame and glory.

I wanted to make my empire bigger. I wanted British slaves, corn, gold and tin.

Think of all those soldiers who have been killed...

LOOKING AT EVIDENCE

A statue of Julius Caesar.

A Roman coin.

The Britons all dye their skin with woad which makes them a blue colour.
They look terrifying in battle.

The Romans could write. Julius Caesar wrote this in <u>Latin</u> over 2,000 years ago.

The Roman army

The Romans had invaded other countries as well as Britain. All these countries made up their empire. The Roman army was the best in the world. It was divided up into legions. Each legion had about 5,000 men. A Roman soldier was called a legionary.

Some soldiers came from countries that the Romans had invaded. They were called auxiliaries. They were not paid as much as the legionaries. Some auxiliaries rode horses, others were archers.

The storming of Maiden Castle

Soon after invading Britain the Romans attacked and defeated a Celtic tribe at the great hill-fort of Maiden Castle.

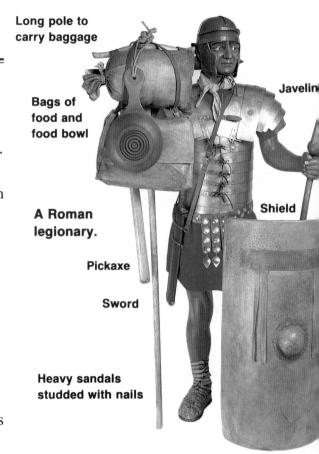

Long pole to carry baggage

Bags of food and food bowl

Javelin

A Roman legionary.

Shield

Pickaxe

Sword

Heavy sandals studded with nails

The Romans used different kinds of war machines such as catapults which fired rocks. Ballistas were giant cross-bows that fired huge arrows.

Legionaries put their shields together to protect themselves from arrows and spears. The shape they made was called a "tortoise".

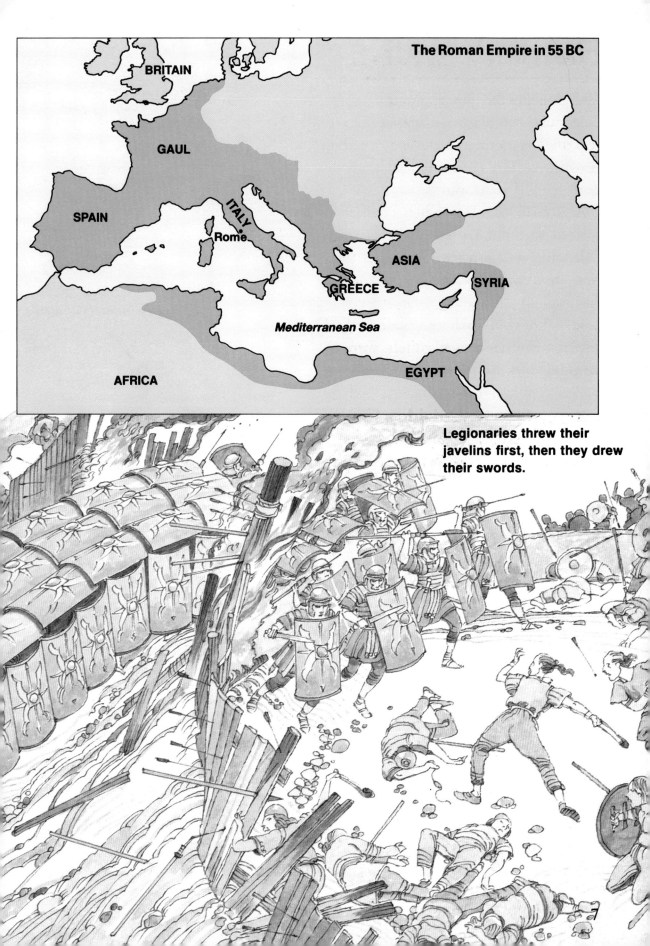

The Roman Empire in 55 BC

BRITAIN

GAUL

SPAIN

ITALY

Rome

ASIA

GREECE

SYRIA

Mediterranean Sea

AFRICA

EGYPT

Legionaries threw their javelins first, then they drew their swords.

Hadrian's Wall

The Romans did not conquer Caledonia, the place we now call Scotland. A fierce tribe called the <u>Picts</u> lived there. The Picts often attacked the Romans and the Celts.

A Roman emperor called Hadrian decided to build a great wall between Caledonia and Britain. He hoped the Picts would not be able to get over this wall.

Ten thousand soldiers usually guarded Hadrian's Wall. They came from all over the Roman Empire.

The wall was often attacked and parts of it destroyed. But for 250 years most people in Roman Britain lived in peace and safety behind it.

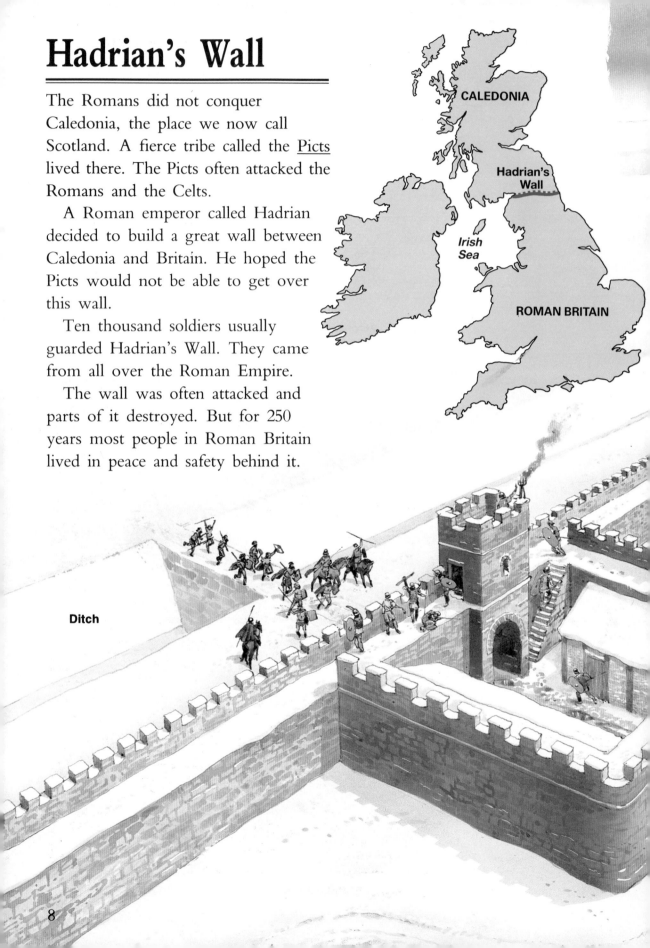

CALEDONIA

Hadrian's Wall

Irish Sea

ROMAN BRITAIN

Ditch

There were 2 signal towers along every mile of the wall.

Every 5 or 6 miles was a fort which could hold hundreds of soldiers.

When the Picts attacked, beacon fires were lit to warn other soldiers along the wall. Soldiers from the forts marched along the road that ran behind the wall to deal with the Picts.

Every mile there was a mile-castle which could hold up to 50 men.

▲ Hadrian's Wall today.

Roman roads and trade

The Romans built the first real roads in Britain. They were so well built that you can still see some of them today. Roman legionaries did most of the building. They had to decide where the best places were to build the roads. This is called surveying.

Sighting pole

Wooden posts marked out the line of the road.

Roman surveyors used a groma to make the road as straight as possible. Smoke from fires in the distance acted as markers.

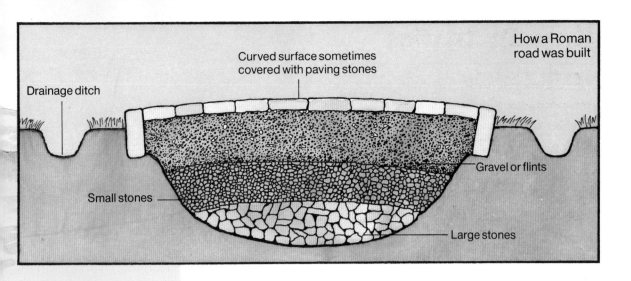

How a Roman road was built

Drainage ditch

Curved surface sometimes covered with paving stones

Gravel or flints

Small stones

Large stones

Why did the Romans build roads?

Good roads helped trade. People could carry goods a long way to sell them. To help travellers, inns and stables were built along the road. Travel was easier and safer than it had been before.

I have come from across the sea to sell things in Britain. I am going to sell wine, olive oil, glass and spices.

I am going to sail across the sea to sell things. I have gold, silver, tin, pots, furs and slaves.

The emperor can send messengers like me to all parts of the empire.

We can march quickly into battle.

A milestone

Roman towns

The Romans built the first real towns in Britain. They thought that people could lead a better life in towns. Some Celts moved to these towns from their small villages.

Roman towns were nearly all built to the same pattern. Streets were laid out in neat, straight lines, like on a chess-board. Buildings were made of stone and brick. Many towns had running water and sewers.

Roman towns

The <u>forum</u> was a place where people could meet and talk. Around the forum were shops which sold clothes, shoes, food, wine, pots and pans, spices and jewellery.

Plan of Roman Silchester

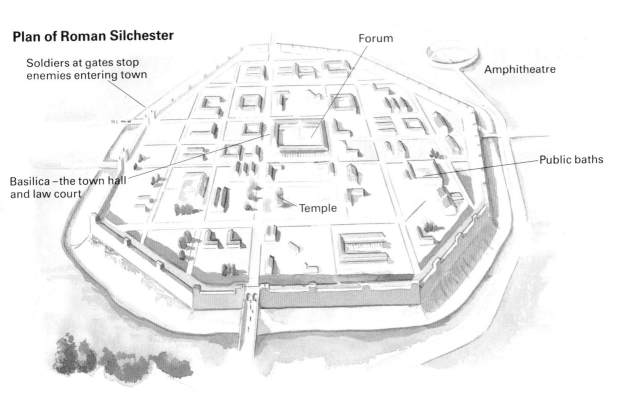

Soldiers at gates stop enemies entering town

Forum

Amphitheatre

Public baths

Basilica – the town hall and law court

Temple

Most Roman shops were small, with just a counter facing the street. Craftspeople often worked at the back of the shop. The shopkeeper usually lived above the shop.

Shops had never existed in Britain before. After the Romans left, there were no more shops in Britain for another 900 years.

▲ **What sort of shop is this?**

Baths and amphitheatres

Every Roman town had one or more public baths and the Romans loved to visit them. There were separate baths for men and women. Children were let in free.

The most famous baths in Britain were in the town of Bath. Here the Romans bathed in hot spring water which they thought had magic powers to cure illnesses.

▲ The hot springs at Bath today.

The Romans did not go to the baths just to get clean. The baths were more like a club. They could spend hours there, sitting around, playing games, talking to friends, eating snacks and swimming.

Plays, games and gladiators

Many towns had open-air arenas or amphitheatres. Visitors could watch wrestling, circuses, concerts and plays.

Romans also liked watching blood-thirsty sports in the amphitheatres called 'the games'. Sometimes wild animals were forced to fight each other. Fights between armed men called <u>gladiators</u> were also popular.

▼ There was no soap in Roman times. To get clean they covered their bodies with oil which they then scraped off with a curved scraper called a strigil.

▼ The Retiarius fought with a trident and net.

▲ The Secutor fought with a shield and sword.

▲ The Roman amphitheatre at St Albans today.

Everyday life in Roman Britain

Life for the rich

Life in Roman Britain was different for rich and poor, young and old, male or female, Roman or Celt. Many rich Celts soon learnt to live like Romans. They were usually called Romano-Britons. They had Roman names and wore Roman clothes.

Children from rich families went to school. They learned <u>Latin</u>, Greek, History, Geography and Arithmetic. Teachers were very strict. Children who did not work hard were beaten.

▲ **Remains of a Roman writing tablet and different kinds of stylus.**

Most schools had only one room. The children wrote on wooden tablets covered with wax using a pen called a 'stylus'. Older children wrote on paper called <u>papyrus</u> with ink pens.

16

Slaves at work in a rich family's kitchen.

Bronze Roman saucepan.

Life for the poor

Most people in Roman Britain were not rich. They did not go to school or learn how to read and write.

There were many slaves, owned by people in the same way that we own pets today. Slaves worked down mines, on farms, and in shops. Many slaves worked in the houses of rich people, cleaning and cooking. Some owners treated their slaves well, others treated them badly.

Slaves could be bought at the market place. They were often people the Romans had captured in wars.

Most Celts did not live like the Romans. They still farmed their lands and lived in wood and mud huts.

A Roman villa

In the countryside, rich Romans and Romano–Britons built new houses called villas. Some villas had many of the things we have in our houses today. They had glass windows, running water, baths, and toilets that flushed. Most villas had a form of central heating called a hypocaust. Floors were built on brick pillars. Hot air from a furnace travelled under the floors and up behind the walls, keeping the rooms warm. The Romans needed hypocausts in chilly Britain.

▼ **This is a model of a living room in a villa. The floor is a mosaic. Mosaic is made from hundreds of pieces of tiny coloured stones set in cement.**

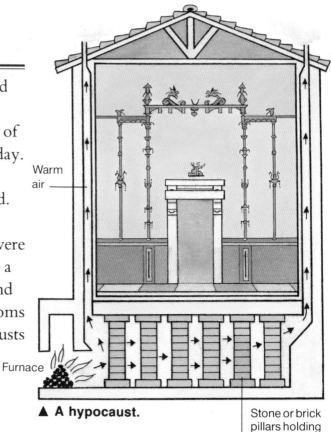

Warm air

Furnace

▲ A hypocaust.

Stone or brick pillars holding up floor

▼ A menu from a Roman feast.

-MENU-

Course I - eggs with rye bread

Course II - oysters

Course III - chicken with garlic

Course IV - stuffed dormice

Course V - roast peacock

Course VI - roast boar

Course VII - pastries

Course VIII - fruit

Course IX - fried thrush

▲ This is how the Roman villa at Lullingstone may have looked.

Rich Romans loved long dinner parties. They lay on couches and ate with their hands.

Religion in Roman times

The Romans believed in many gods and goddesses. Many of the Roman gods were the same as those of the Greeks, but they had different names. Some of our months are named after Roman gods.

Some Romans had their own family god or goddess. Families often had a special place in the house where they placed gifts of food or wine for their god.

The Romans built temples to their gods and goddesses. Some emperors were also worshipped as gods.

▲ Statue of Mars.

▼ This is a model of the temple of the Emperor Claudius at Colchester.

Roman gods and goddesses

JUNO
GODDESS OF WOMEN AND CHILDREN

JUPITER
KING OF THE GODS

MARS
GOD OF WAR

VENUS
GODDESS OF LOVE AND BEAUTY

Celtic religion

The Celts also believed in many gods and goddesses. Their priests were called Druids. They held religious ceremonies in the forests. The Romans hated the Druids and killed many of them. But many Celtic and Roman gods were very similar. Celts and Romans often worshipped together.

Christianity

Some Romans were Christians. They believed that there was only one god. Other Romans hated them. Some Emperors had many Christians killed. Despite this, more and more Romans became Christian. Finally, the Romans decided that Christianity was the true religion and they did not allow anyone to worship any other gods.

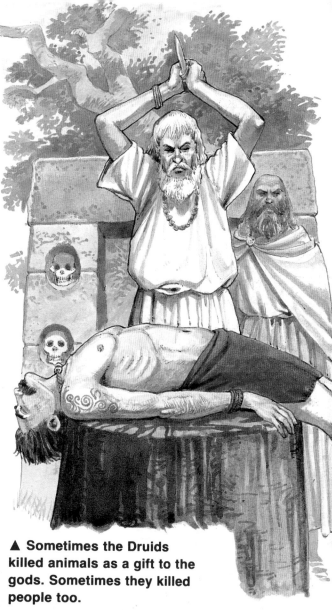

▲ Sometimes the Druids killed animals as a gift to the gods. Sometimes they killed people too.

▲ This Roman mosaic shows the head of Christ.

21

The Anglo-Saxons

For over 300 years, Britain was part of the Roman Empire. Then, other tribes of people began to attack the Romans from all sides. They wanted to steal land and riches from the Romans. Even Rome was under attack.

North Sea

ANGLES

CALEDONIA

PICTS

IRELAND

SCOTS

SAXONS

1 The Romans decided to leave Britain. Some Britons were happy to see them go while others were sad.

3 Enemy tribes called <u>Scots</u> sailed from Ireland. <u>Picts</u> came over Hadrian's Wall. They attacked the Britons.

2 Roman towns and villas fell into ruins. Roads were not repaired.

4 Across the sea, in what now call Germany, Denma and the Netherlands, lived tribes of Angles and Saxo The Britons paid these Anglo-Saxons to come an help them.

5 The Anglo-Saxons defeated the Picts and Scots. But when the Britons asked them to go back home they refused. They attacked and defeated the Britons. They built homes and settled in Britain.

Once the Romans had gone, there was no one to defend Britain.

Why did the Anglo-Saxons invade?

Britain is richer than Germany. I wanted to steal and kill.

We are farmers. Britain has a lot of good land.

The Britons asked us to come and fight for them.

LOOKING AT EVIDENCE

Only a few Anglo-Saxons could write so we don't know much about Britain at this time. This period is sometimes called <u>The Dark Ages</u>.

This Anglo-Saxon ship was dug up at Sutton Hoo. Many precious objects and weapons were found inside.

Some bodies of Anglo-Saxons have been found preserved in peat bogs.

THERE WAS A LOT OF FIGHTING. BRITISH TOWNS WERE SOON FULL OF BITS OF BODIES.

A British monk called Gildas wrote in <u>Latin</u> about the terrible battles between the Anglo-Saxons and Britons.

Anglo-Saxon kingdoms

The Anglo-Saxons took over much of Britain. They called the land they occupied 'Angle-land' or England. Sometimes, the Britons let the Anglo-Saxons have some of their land, other times they fought back. Soon the Britons ruled only Cumbria, Wales and Cornwall. Many Britons who stayed in England became slaves of the Anglo-Saxons.

The Anglo-Saxons also fought with each other. Their lands became divided into several kingdoms which were often at war with each other.

Anglo-Saxon kingdoms in the 7th century

Northumbria
Mercia
East Anglia
Essex
Kent
Wessex
Sussex

Sailing across the North Sea to Britain was dangerous. Many Anglo-Saxon ships were simple rowing boats with no sail.

One man steered the ship with a rudder.

24

This large Anglo-Saxon helmet was found in the Sutton Hoo ship. It may have had soft padding inside like a crash helmet.

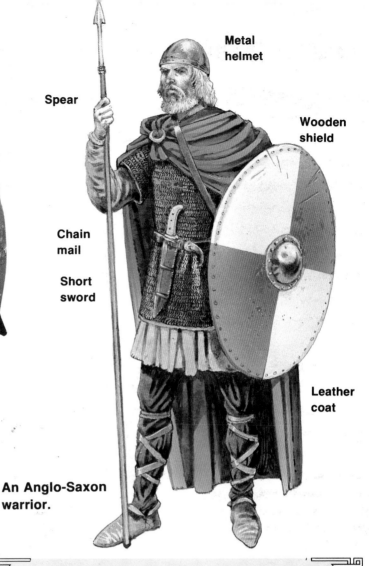

Spear

Metal helmet

Wooden shield

Chain mail

Short sword

Leather coat

An Anglo-Saxon warrior.

The ships were long and narrow. The Anglo-Saxons could row them up shallow rivers to settle in Britain.

Myths and Legends

Some Britons fought hard against the Anglo-Saxons. Storytellers later told of a great British leader called Arthur who won many battles. There are many stories about King Arthur and his knights of the Round Table but it is unlikely that these stories are true. It is not even certain that King Arthur ever lived.

Anglo-Saxon villages

The Anglo-Saxons were more like the Celts than the Romans. They lived in small villages surrounded by a wooden fence. They did not build in stone. Their houses were made out of mud, wood and straw.

In the middle of an Anglo-Saxon village was the Great Hall. Halls were like big barns with no windows. The floor was covered with rushes or straw. The Anglo-Saxons loved eating and feasting. They enjoyed listening to riddles, poems and stories.

▲ **An Anglo-Saxon village.**

Inside an Anglo-Saxon Hall.

Myths and Legends

One famous Anglo-Saxon story tells of the hero Beowulf. He saved his people from a monster called Grendel. He also killed Grendel's horrible mother.

Can you solve this riddle? My nose is pointed. I crawl along and dig in the ground. I go as I am guided by my lord who walks stooping behind me. He lifts me and presses me on and sows in my track.

Anglo-Saxon people

Thanes

The thane was the most important man in the village. He lived in the Great Hall with his family. He made sure everyone obeyed the law and led his people in battles against enemy tribes.

Slaves

Slaves were often criminals or prisoners captured in war. They did not own their own house or land. They slept on the floor of the Great Hall.

▲ Rich thanes wore fine clothes and valuable jewellery.

▼ A picture from Anglo-Saxon times showing churls ploughing their field.

Slaves wore simple clothes and often did not have any shoes.

28

This is what a churl's house may have looked like inside. The house had no windows or chimney, just a hole in the roof. The floor was covered with straw.

Thatched roof

Woven beehive

Churls

Churls were farmers who owned their own land. There were no shops, so the churls had to work hard to grow all their own food. They ploughed the land, grew barley, and kept animals. Children had to help on the farm or work in the home. There were no schools.

Churls used the barley to make ale or bread. They spent a lot of time spinning and weaving to make clothes.

There were no doctors or hospitals. Some churls knew which were the best herbs to use, like medicine, when someone was ill. Few people lived past the age of 50. Many children died before their first birthday.

Anglo-Saxons and Christianity

The Anglo-Saxons were pagans. They worshipped many gods like Tiw, Woden, Thunor and Frigg.

In the 7th <u>century</u>, Roman and Celtic monks <u>converted</u> many of the Anglo-Saxons to Christianity. Gradually most of Britain became Christian. But there were differences between the Celtic and Roman Churches.

How do you think Tuesday, Wednesday, Thursday and Friday got their names? Here's a clue. Tuesday is the day of Tiw.

The Christian conversions

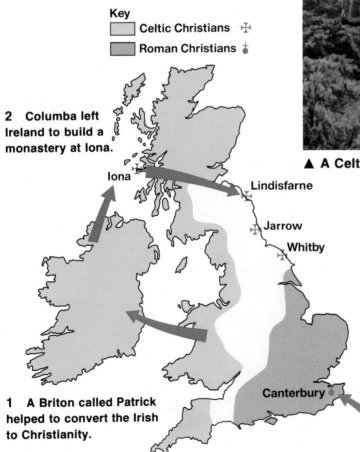

Key
- Celtic Christians ☩
- Roman Christians ⚰

2 Columba left Ireland to build a monastery at Iona.

Iona

Lindisfarne

Jarrow

Whitby

Canterbury

1 A Briton called Patrick helped to convert the Irish to Christianity.

▲ **A Celtic cross**

4 Aidan travelled from Iona to set up a monastery at Lindisfarne. Monks from Lindisfarne went out preaching and converting people all over northern England.

3 In 597 <u>AD</u> Pope Gregory sent Augustine to convert the Anglo-Saxons to Christianity. Augustine built a church at Canterbury, which soon became the most important church in England. Augustine became the first Archbishop of Canterbury.

Monasteries and manuscripts

In the 7th and 8th centuries, many churches and monasteries were built. Schools were set up to train boys and girls to be monks and nuns. Many monks and nuns could read and write. They spent a lot of time copying out books by hand. They wrote with a quill pen on parchment made from animal skin.

Soon, there were many famous Anglo-Saxon scholars. The most famous was Bede who lived in a monastery at Jarrow.

The Synod of Whitby

In 664, King Oswy of Northumbria held a meeting (called a Synod) at Whitby. After a great debate he decided that Northumbria would follow the rules of the Roman Church. Most Anglo-Saxons soon obeyed the Pope.

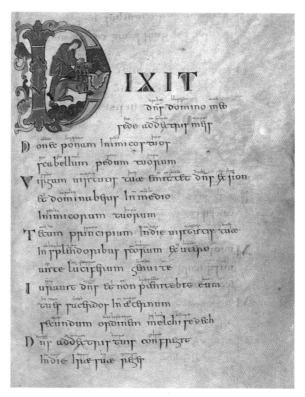

▲ A page from an Anglo-Saxon manuscript.

Anglo-Saxon laws

Anglo-Saxon kings were expected to keep law and order. They had the power to make new laws or cancel old ones. They made new laws with the help of the <u>Witan</u>. The Witan was made up of the king's friends and the chief men in the kingdom.

Thanes tried to make sure no one broke the law. Those who did were brought before a village court called a moot.

There were no prisons. People found guilty of serious crimes were beaten or had their hands or feet cut off. Some were hanged.

An Anglo-Saxon picture showing a man pleading his case before the king.

Wergild

If you hurt or killed someone, you had to pay money to that person or to their family. If you could not pay, you became their slave. This money was called wergild.

If you killed a thane, you had to pay a wergild of 1,200 shillings. If you killed a churl, it was only 200 shillings.

Every part of the body had a wergild price.

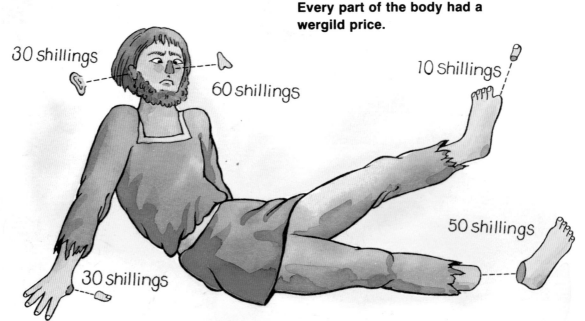

30 shillings

60 shillings

10 shillings

50 shillings

30 shillings

Oath-helpers

Some people said they were not guilty of the crimes they were accused of. You could prove your innocence if you could find enough people who would swear an oath that you were not guilty.

Trial by ordeal

If accused people could not find enough oath-helpers they had to suffer trial by ordeal. The Anglo-Saxons thought that God would protect an innocent person.

Sometimes the accused person had to hold a very hot object. Their hands were then bandaged. If after three days their hands had begun to heal they were believed to be innocent.

Ordeal by water

The accused person was tied up and thrown into a pond.

If he floated he was believed to be guilty.

If he sank he was believed to be innocent (but he might have drowned by the time he was pulled out).

Ordeal by heat

The accused person had to carry a red-hot iron bar for three paces.

In another ordeal by heat the accused person had to put their hand into boiling water to pick up a stone.

Offa's Dyke

In the 8th century, Mercia was the strongest Anglo-Saxon kingdom. King Offa was the greatest Mercian king. A Welsh monk wrote that Offa "struck terror into all the kings and lands around him." Offa called himself King of all the English. Several other Anglo-Saxon kings swore to obey him.

Offa was not friendly with the Welsh. Welsh raiders often stole cattle and slaves from Mercia. Offa attacked but failed to conquer Wales.

Finally Offa ordered a great dyke to be built between Mercia and Wales. A dyke is a high mound of earth behind a ditch.

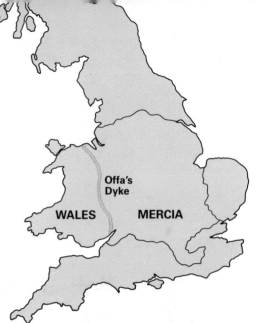

Offa's Dyke stretched for over 100 miles. Thousands of people were needed to build the dyke. The earth wall was 25 feet high in places. There may have been a wooden fence and look-out towers on top.

We still do not know why Offa ordered the dyke to be built. He may have built the dyke to show exactly where his kingdom ended. Perhaps he thought the dyke would stop Welsh raids into Mercia.

Offa's coins

Archaeologists have found many silver and gold coins with Offa's picture and name on them. They were the finest of all Anglo-Saxon coins and were used throughout England. We do not know if Offa really looked like this. The picture on this coin may just have been copied from a picture on a foreign coin.

▲ Offa's Dyke today.

The Vikings

At the end of the 8th century, fierce raiders began to attack Britain. They came from Denmark, Norway and Sweden. These people are known as the Vikings. They attacked villages and churches near the coast, then they returned home with their stolen riches.

▶ In 793, Viking raiders attacked the famous abbey of Lindisfarne. They killed many of the monks.

Soon there were more and more raids on Britain.

▼ In 865, a large Viking army led by Ivar the Boneless invaded England. The Vikings conquered East Anglia, Northumbria and Mercia. The only Anglo-Saxon kingdom to hold out was Wessex.

There was plenty to steal from the churches and monasteries!

Why did the Vikings invade?

I wanted to fight and steal.

I'm a farmer. There was not enough good farm land in Norway.

I wanted to trade.

LOOKING AT EVIDENCE

A Viking skating boot.

A Viking board game.

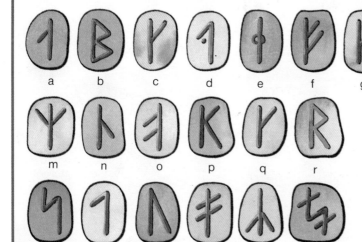

a b c d e f g h i k l

m n o p q r

Many Vikings could read and write but they seldom wrote on paper. They carved letters called <u>runes</u> onto stones, wood and weapons.

s t u v w x y z

Viking ships

For 300 years, the Vikings were the finest shipbuilders and sailors in Europe. They made their best ships out of oak. At least 12 trees were needed to make one ship. The shipbuilders used very simple tools but they built ships which could sail great distances across rough seas.

Vikings sailed east to Russia, south to the Mediterranean Sea and west to Britain. Some Vikings even sailed to Iceland, Greenland and America.

▲ **A Viking longship in a museum in Norway.**

Ships for war

Viking warships or longships were narrow and fast. They could sail up shallow rivers.

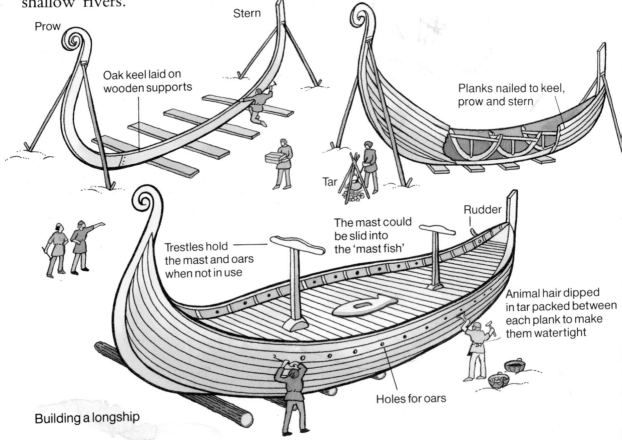

Prow

Stern

Oak keel laid on wooden supports

Planks nailed to keel, prow and stern

Tar

The mast could be slid into the 'mast fish'

Rudder

Trestles hold the mast and oars when not in use

Animal hair dipped in tar packed between each plank to make them watertight

Holes for oars

Building a longship

The helmsman steered the ship with the rudder. He used the sun and stars to find his way.

The crew spent a lot of time bailing out water. If the wind was not strong the men rowed the ship with oars.

Ships for trade

The Vikings also built slower but stronger ships called knorrs. These were used by traders and Viking settlers who were moving to new lands.

Life at sea was very uncomfortable. There was no shelter from the cold and the rain. The crew ate cold fish or meat and drank from barrels of water.

Alfred the Great

Alfred is the only English king who is called "the Great". He was the youngest son of the Saxon King of Wessex. Alfred had three older brothers and seemed to have little chance of becoming king. But his father and brothers died and, in 871, he became King of Wessex. Alfred had to fight many battles to stop the Vikings taking over Wessex.

The leader of the Vikings was called Guthrum. He attacked Alfred at Christmas when most of his soldiers were working on their farms. Alfred had to hide in a forest and wait until spring came. Then he gathered his men together and defeated the Vikings.

Alfred and Guthrum agreed that they should each rule half of England. The land the Vikings ruled was called the Danelaw.

▲ **Statue of Alfred in Winchester, his capital.**

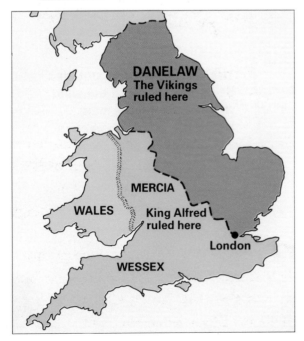

A silver penny showing Alfred. We do not know what Alfred really looked like.

Myths and Legends

There are many famous stories about Alfred. One tells how he was given a precious book by his mother after he learned all the stories in it by heart. Another tells how he was hit over the head by a swineherd's wife because he burnt her cakes. These stories are probably not true.

▶ A 16th century picture of Alfred burning the cakes.

Was Alfred great?

Alfred was not just a good soldier. This is what Bishop Asser wrote about him. Bishop Asser was a good friend of Alfred's.

Alfred built finer buildings than ever before. He was very religious, going to church by day and night. He gave a lot of money to the poor. He was nice to everybody.

Alfred set up a school at Winchester for the sons of his most important families.

Alfred took the best laws from other kingdoms and had a new book of laws written. He made the army stronger and built many ships in case the Vikings attacked again.

Alfred died in 899 <u>AD</u>. He had not driven the Vikings out of England but he was the only Saxon king to stop them invading all of England.

Viking York

York was the capital of Viking England. Thousands of Vikings settled there. They called the town Jorvik. In Viking times, Jorvik was one of the biggest towns in Europe.

In 1976 <u>archaeologists</u> began to dig up Coppergate, an old Viking street in York. They found 15,000 small objects and the remains of buildings. The Viking street of Coppergate has now been rebuilt at the Jorvik Viking centre.

This woman is weaving cloth on a loom. Viking farmers spent much of their time preparing food, spinning and weaving, and looking after their animals.

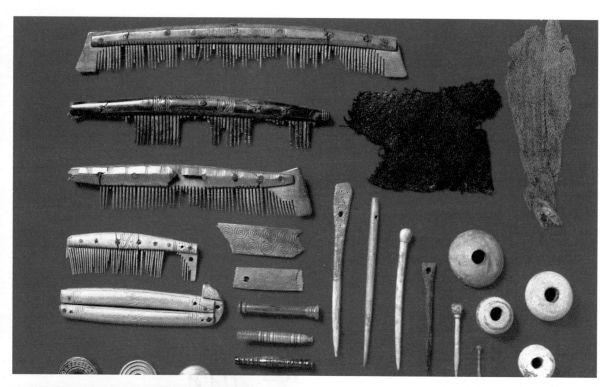

These are Viking combs and pins made from horn and bone. The pieces of cloth are from a Viking loom.

You can also see round stone spinning weights. These were tied onto the bottom of threads on the loom to hold them straight.

This craftsman is an antler worker. He carved antlers into combs, pins or spoons.

Life in Jorvik

These are models of Viking people from the Jorvik centre. Viking Jorvik was a very busy town full of wooden houses, warehouses and workshops. Traders sailed to Jorvik to buy and sell their goods. Skilled craftspeople made weapons, jewellery and tools.

Houses were built very close together. In the middle of each house was a big open hearth. If a house caught fire it could easily spread to other houses. Archaeologists have found remains of burnt houses in Coppergate.

Viking people and gods

The Vikings and Anglo-Saxons were very similar. They spoke a similar language, they wore similar clothes and they both liked feasting and drinking. Rich Vikings lived in Great Halls, just like Anglo-Saxon thanes.

Vikings liked to play board games, like chess, and sports like wrestling and swimming.

They cared a great deal about how they looked. They washed regularly, combed their hair, and wore brightly coloured clothes and as much jewellery as they could afford.

▼ This model shows the inside of a Viking house. Most houses had only one room which was often shared with farm animals. The houses had no windows or chimneys.

▲ This Jorvik model shows the food the Vikings ate. Archaeologists found food remains when they dug up Viking rubbish tips in Coppergate.

The gods of Asgard

The Vikings worshipped many gods. They believed that their gods lived in the sky at a place called Asgard. Each god had his own hall. Odin's hall was called Valhalla. Viking warriors believed that if they died bravely in battle they would be taken to Valhalla. At Valhalla, the brave warriors spent their time feasting with the gods.

The Vikings told stories, called sagas, about their gods. In these sagas the gods had many adventures and often played tricks on each other.

As Viking settlers began to marry English people, and accept English customs, most of them became Christians.

Viking gods and goddesses

ODIN
LORD OF THE GODS AND GOD OF WAR

FREYJA
GODDESS OF LOVE, BATTLE AND DEATH

THOR
SON OF ODIN GOD OF THE SKY

The Kingdom of England

The Anglo-Saxons and Vikings fought many battles after Alfred the Great died. Alfred's grandson was called Athelstan. He forced all the Vikings in England to accept him as king. For the first time an Anglo-Saxon king was the ruler of all of England. The rulers of Scotland and Wales also promised to obey Athelstan, so he was almost King of all Britain.

At the end of the 10th century, large Viking armies attacked England again. The Anglo-Saxon king Ethelred the Unready was afraid of the Vikings. He paid them great sums of money not to invade England. But the Vikings returned and defeated the Anglo-Saxons.

▲ In 1016, a Viking called Canute became King of England. This picture of Canute was drawn when he was King.

King Ethelred gave the Vikings gold and silver coins to stop them invading. This money was called Danegeld.

Britain in the 11th century

In some ways, life in Britain was not very different from life in Celtic times. Most people still lived in wood and mud huts in small villages. All the grand Roman buildings lay in ruins.

But some things had changed. Lots of different groups of people had come and settled in Britain. British people were now a mix of Celt, Roman, Anglo-Saxon and Viking.

Almost everyone was Christian. Many priests, monks and nuns could read and write.

England was now one kingdom, ruled by one king, and most people spoke English.

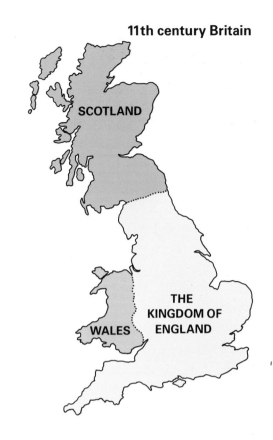

11th century Britain

SCOTLAND

WALES

THE KINGDOM OF ENGLAND

INVADERS

In 1066, William of Normandy invaded England and killed the Anglo-Saxon king Harold at the Battle of Hastings. England was not finished with invaders yet!

Glossary

These words are <u>underlined</u> in this book.

AD
This is short for "Anno Domini" which means "from the year of our Lord" or after the birth of Christ.

Archaeologists
People who have been trained to excavate (dig up) historical sites. They study the objects they find and tell us what life in the past may have been like.

BC
This is short for "Before Christ".

Britain
England, Scotland and Wales.

Century
A hundred years. The 1st century was from the birth of Christ to 100 AD.

Converted
People who are converted to a religion are persuaded to change their beliefs.

Danelaw
The part of England taken over by the Vikings in the late 9th century. Most Vikings in England came from Denmark. Danelaw was the place where people obeyed Danish law.

Dark Ages
The name often given for the period 400-700 AD.

Forum
A market place at the centre of most Roman towns.

Gladiators
People trained to fight to the death in Roman amphitheatres.

Latin
The language spoken and written by the Romans.

Papyrus
Paper the Romans wrote on made from an Egyptian reed.

Picts
A tribe of people who lived in Scotland in Roman and Anglo-Saxon times.

Runes
Viking letters made up of straight lines only, so they were easier to carve onto wood or stone.

Scholar
Someone who has learned a lot from books.

Scots
An Irish tribe that began to settle in Scotland in the 4th and 5th centuries.

Witan
A group of wise men that advised an Anglo-Saxon king.